T0014215

MINECRAFT
MASTER BUILDER
ANCIENT WONDERS

Published in 2022 by Mortimer Children's
An Imprint of Welbeck Children's Limited,
part of Welbeck Publishing Group.
Based in London and Sydney.
www.welbeckpublishing.com

Design and layout © Welbeck Children's Limited 2022
Text copyright © Welbeck Children's Limited 2022

ISBN: 978 1 83935 098 6

Models built by: Ben Westwood

The publishers would like to thank the following sources for
their kind permission to reproduce the pictures in this
book.

SHUTTERSTOCK: /Anton_Ivanov: 6B; /TTstudio: 7T; /
Abdoabdalla: 7BR; /Zbigniew Guzowski: 8BL; /ribazprudu:
8R; /Dan Breckwoldt: 9T; /moonfish8: 9BR; / agsaz: 9BL; /
Michael Rosskothen: 24TL; /Elena Terletskaya: 24BL; /
Elenarts: 24BR; /neftali: 24BR; /Doug Walters: 25TR; /
Lefteris Papaulakis: 25TL; /Photos BrianScantlebury: 25BR;
/S-F: 25BL; / chuyuss: 40TL; /Sean Pavone: 40TR; /
aphotostory: 40-41B/Zhao jiankang: 41T; /Mario Savoia:
41BR; /Anna Om: 56TR; /saiko3p: 56B; /milosk50: 57T; /
Natalya Erofeeva: 57BL; /Peter Maerky: 57BR; /Nort: 71

Designed, written and packaged by: Dynamo Limited
Design Manager: Sam James
Editorial Manager: Joff Brown
Production: Melanie Robertson

Printed in Dongguan, China
10 9 8 7 6 5 4 3

All game information correct as of March 2021

MINECRAFT MASTER BUILDER

ANCIENT WONDERS

MORTIMER

CONTENTS

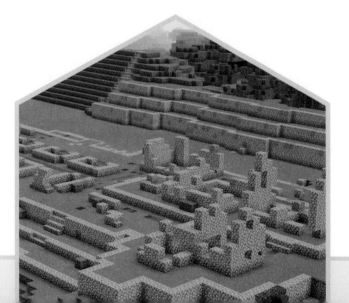

WELCOME TO MINECRAFT ANCIENT WONDERS

Welcome to your go-to guide to building the Ancient Wonders of the World. Inside, you'll find out about temples, tombs, palaces, and sculptures, from China to Greece. Get ready to travel back in time across continents and cultures, before getting the chance to recreate them for yourself! This awesome book is jam-packed with step-by-steps and tips to help you on your way. So, what are you waiting for?

New to Minecraft?

If you are yet to experience the joys of Minecraft, then you're in for a big treat. It's a good idea to familiarize yourself with the way the game works and play around with the basic game play before you dive into building. If you take some time to get to grips with Minecraft, you'll have more fun when it's time to get creative.

Doing more

This book has an epic selection of ancient builds from around the world, but why stop there? Once you've polished up your Minecraft skills using our step-by-step guides, you can try your hand at building anything you like. You could design your own temples and palaces—or even blend two World Wonders together. Imagine what the Colossus of Rhodes would look like on top of the Sphinx!

GIANT WILD GOOSE PAGODA

PARTHENON

STAYING SAFE ONLINE

Minecraft is one of the most popular games on the planet because it combines amazing building with fun. However, the most important part of the game is to stay safe when you are online.

Below are our tips for keeping safe:

- Tell a trusted adult what you're doing, and ask before downloading anything
- Speak to a trusted adult if you are worried about anything
- Turn off chat
- Find a child-friendly server
- Only screenshare with real-life friends
- Watch out for viruses and malware
- Set a game-play time limit

GREAT PYRAMID AND SPHINX

HOW MANY BLOCKS?

When you're building, keep an eye out for the symbols below. They will tell you how many blocks you need in each part of the build.

 Blocks

 Slabs

ANCIENT EGYPT

Prepare to explore an ancient land known for pharaohs, temples, and underground tombs.

Obelisk

In Ancient Egypt, obelisks were impressive stone pillars found guarding the entrances of temples. Symbolic carvings, known as hieroglyphs, can be seen on all four sides of an obelisk. Traditional obelisks were monolithic (carved from a single stone) and made from granite. Carving such an impressive stone would have been a huge challenge in Ancient Egypt.

DID YOU KNOW?

Obelisks were monuments that honored Egyptian gods and the dead.

Karnak Temple

This 61-acre (25-hectare) temple complex is one of the largest Egyptian temples that still exists today. The epic Karnak Temple took over 2,000 years to build. Inside, there are various shrines, statues, and carvings dedicated to the god Amun-Re, who was chief of the Egyptian gods. A temple this size needed a huge number of guards, servants, and priests to run it—over 80,000 altogether!

Abu Simbel

Abu Simbel is made up of two temples carved out of a cliff. This ancient temple complex was built during the reign of an Egyptian king named Ramses II. The temples feature extravagant carvings of gods and intricate detailing, so it's no wonder that they took 20 years to build! It is believed that the temples were built to symbolize Egypt's power.

Valley of the Kings

Large and complex tombs were common in Ancient Egyptian times, but none was quite as famous as this one. The Valley of the Kings was a collection of underground tombs that became the burial place of infamous pharaohs, such as Tutankhamun. Pharaohs were buried here along with their finest treasures, clothes, and enough food and drink for feasts in the afterlife!

Temple of Luxor

Luxor translates as "the palaces". At the entrance to the temple, there were six royal statues and two obelisks. Only one of the obelisks remains—the other is in Paris! The Temple of Luxor is near the Nile River and also the Karnak Temple, and an avenue of sphinxes links them together (now that's some build!)

DIFFICULTY: EASY   BUILD TIME: 1 HOUR

EGYPTIAN OBELISK

Get ready to build an obelisk! These impressive pillars would have been found at the entrances of Ancient Egyptian temples.

MATERIALS

STEP 1

First, dig out a square that is 13 blocks long and 13 blocks wide.

Dig out the middle, too!

STEP 2

Next, mark the center point by removing the central block, as shown. Fill in the rest of the square using **chiseled quartz blocks**, until it looks like this.

STEP 3

Dig out three rows of blocks on each side of the square—these rows should be gradually one block shorter, as shown below. Fill in these four new sections with **chiseled quartz blocks**.

STEP 4

Next, build up the pillar from the center point you made in Step 2. The pillar should be 32 blocks high and made from **smooth sandstone**.

STEP 5

Next, it's time to add a base to the tower. Use **sandstone blocks** to make a square that has five blocks on each side.

STEP 6

Build up the base by adding two more layers of **sandstone blocks**. It should now be three layers high and look like this.

Sandstone stairs

Layer of cut sandstone blocks

STEP 7

Add **sandstone stairs** that go all the way around the bottom of the base. Then, you will need four **chiseled stone brick blocks**. Add one of these to each corner of the base. Knock out one block of the pillar (in the center), and add a layer of **cut sandstone blocks** on the top to join up the four **chiseled stone brick blocks**.

Chiseled stone brick blocks

STEP 8

On top of this, add a layer of **sandstone blocks**. Make sure that this layer is smaller than the one below it, as shown below.

STEP 9

Next, you need to make the central pillar wider. To do this, you will need more **smooth sandstone blocks**. Build the pillar outward, until it looks like this.

STEP 10

At the top of the obelisk, add some **smooth sandstone stairs**. Then, add a **smooth sandstone block** right at the top. You can now see the obelisk really taking shape.

STEP 11

You have your main structure, so now it's all about adding the finishing touches. To do this, dig out a row of blocks on all four edges of the tower, like this.

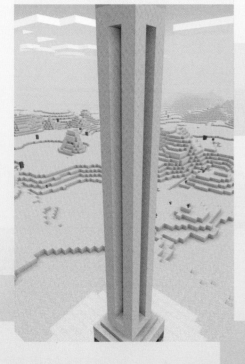

STEP 12

To make your obelisk carvings, simply fill in the gaps that you made in Step 11 using **chiseled sandstone blocks**.

DID YOU KNOW?

Although there are many theories, no one knows exactly how obelisks were built.

KARNAK TEMPLE

It doesn't get much grander than the Karnak Temple.
What a place to begin your temple and shrine-building skills!

MATERIALS

STEP 1

Grab some **cut sandstone** to make a rectangle that is six blocks wide, 12 blocks long, and two blocks high. This is the first plinth for your statue to stand on.

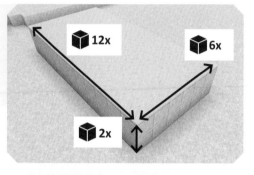

STEP 2

Repeat Step 1 to make 16 plinths. Arrange them in two rows of eight, like this, and have a space of two blocks between each, with a 30-block-wide gap in the middle!

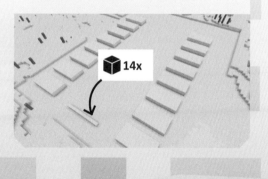

STEP 3

Then, create a path down the middle of the two rows using **quartz brick blocks**. The path should be 14 blocks wide.

Karnak temple is built within 250 acres (100 hectares) of religious buildings, including chapels, obelisks, and temples.

STEP 4

Use **smooth sandstone** to build up the legs of your first statue. These should be four blocks wide, six blocks high, and two blocks deep.

STEP 5

Place four **cut sandstone blocks** along the bottom, like this. Then, use four **smooth sandstone slabs** in front of them to create feet.

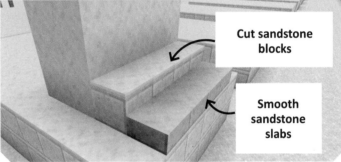

Cut sandstone blocks

Smooth sandstone slabs

STEP 6

Add one layer that is six **sandstone blocks** high, and then put a layer of **cut sandstone blocks** in front of that. This will become the torso.

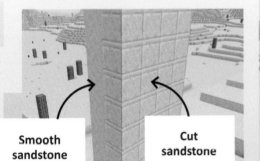

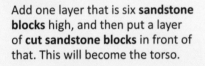

Smooth sandstone

Cut sandstone

Smooth sandstone stairs

STEP 7

Next, use **smooth sandstone blocks** to create the shape below. This will be the statue's arms and hands.

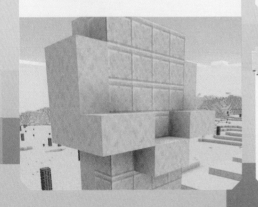

STEP 8

To create the folded arms detail, try using **smooth sandstone stairs** as shown in the picture.

STEP 9

It's time to build the statue's head. Use **smooth sandstone blocks** in a square that is two blocks high and two wide. Add **smooth sandstone slabs** to add detail to the top of the statue's head and shoulders.

STEP 10

At the back of the statue, add **sandstone blocks**, as shown. This section should be 12 blocks high and two blocks wide.

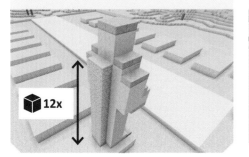

STEP 11

Behind this, create a pillar using **sandstone blocks**. The pillar should be 16 blocks high, four blocks wide, and six blocks deep.

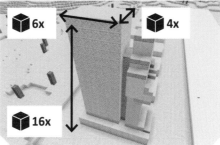

STEP 12

Now that you know the building process, you will need to repeat it on all of your plinths, until your build looks like the picture below.

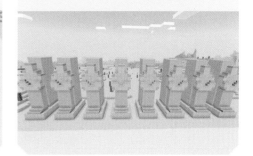

STEP 13

At one end of your statues, build two rows of 13 blocks as a marker (use any blocks you like). Now start to build a wall that is 13 blocks away from the statues, like this. Use **sandstone blocks** to make the wall 19 blocks high. It should be as wide as the whole width of your build so far.

13x as markers

STEP 14

Repeat Step 13 at the other end, but this time you only need to leave a two-block space between the statues and the wall, as shown.

STEP 15

Now connect these ends up by building a **sandstone block** wall all the way around your build. Make the wall two blocks deep by adding a second layer to the outside.

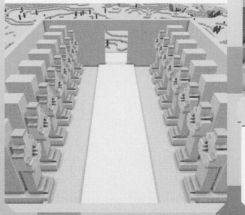

STEP 16

Next, you need to build a roof. This should be three blocks deep and connect the pillars to the outside wall that you just built.

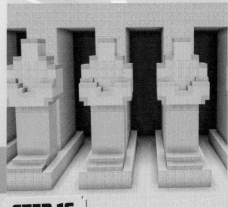

STEP 17

Repeat this along both rows of statues. Then, do the same to the back end, but leave the front one as it is (the front of the temple has the bigger gap).

STEP 18

You can now replace your markers from Step 13 with a layer of **quartz bricks** that is six blocks deep. Add a layer of cut sandstone that is four blocks deep.

You can remove the markers now.

STEP 19

Create two pillars from **sandstone blocks**. The first should be one block in from the corridor. Then, leave a space of 10 blocks and create a second pillar, like this. These pillars should be 16 blocks high.

 1x gap from corridor

STEP 20

Do the same thing on the right-hand side, and then join up the pillars to the rest of roof. It should now look like this.

STEP 21

Use **cut sandstone blocks** and **smooth sandstone slabs** to make feet at the base of your pillars.

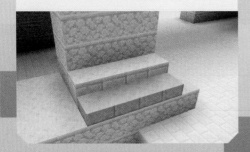

STEP 22

To build up the front of your pillar, start with five **smooth sandstone blocks**. Then, add five **sandstone blocks** on top, as shown.

STEP 23

Now use a combination of **smooth sandstone** and **smooth sandstone stairs** to create arm shapes—just as you did on the first statues.

STEP 24

Use **smooth sandstone** and **smooth sandstone slabs** to create its head and shoulders. Then, simply repeat this for the other pillars.

STEP 25

Add a wall of **cut sandstone blocks** to connect your two statues. The wall only needs to be two blocks deep and three blocks high.

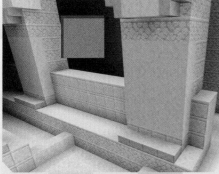

STEP 26

Sandstone stairs are a great way to add detail to the wall. Try this out on both sides.

STEP 27

To decorate the doorways, try using a combination of **cut sandstone** and **chiseled sandstone**. Your temple is complete!

ABU SIMBEL

You'll need excellent statue-making skills to create these two stunning temples that make up one of Egypt's most famous sites.

MATERIALS

STEP 1

First of all, it's important to clear a big space. For this build, you will need an area that is 75 blocks wide and at least 25 blocks deep.

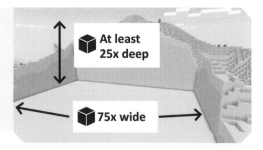

At least 25x deep

75x wide

STEP 2

Use **chiseled red sandstone** to make a ledge across the back. It should be 75 blocks wide, five blocks high, and 17 blocks deep.

STEP 3

On top of this, use **cut red sandstone** to make a seat for the first statue. It should be 13 blocks wide, 12 blocks high, and eight blocks deep.

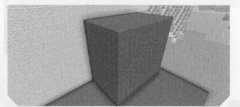

The temples have been carved from solid rock. They can be found along the Nile River.

STEP 4

Next, grab some **smooth red sandstone** to make these shapes for feet. Leave a gap of one block at the end of each foot, like this.

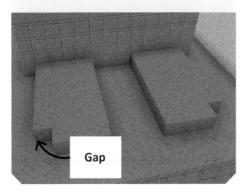

Gap

STEP 5

You'll need more **smooth red sandstone** to create the legs. Build them in graduated columns, so that they look curved.

STEP 6

Use **smooth red sandstone slabs** along with **smooth red sandstone stairs** to give the feet more definition, as shown below.

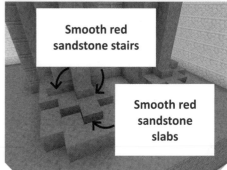

Smooth red sandstone stairs

Smooth red sandstone slabs

STEP 7

You can then create these upper-leg shapes by using **smooth red sandstone blocks** as shown below.

4x

3x

STEP 8

Then, build this shape on top of both legs, using **smooth red sandstone**. Use these measurements to get it right.

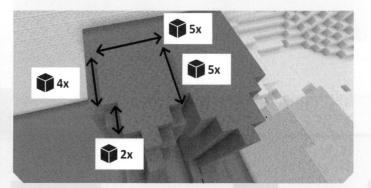

5x

5x

4x

2x

STEP 9

Now add **smooth red sandstone stairs** along the edge, like this. Be sure to do this on both sides.

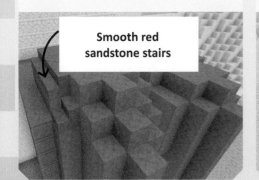

Smooth red sandstone stairs

STEP 10

Create a frame for the torso from **smooth red sandstone**. Build it up so that it is 12 blocks high.

STEP 11

When you're happy with the frame, fill it in using **smooth red sandstone** until it looks like this.

STEP 12

Carefully knock out a ridge seven blocks high, up the edge of the torso. Repeat this on the other side, so that it is symmetrical.

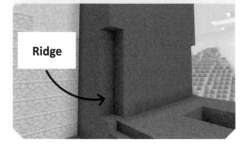

Ridge

STEP 13

Knock out the bottom area of blocks (see 1), then the back ones (see 2), and then the top corners (see 3). Do this on both sides.

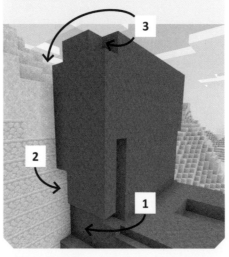

3

2

1

STEP 14

For the arm, add another layer of the same shape, underneath as shown. Do the same on both sides.

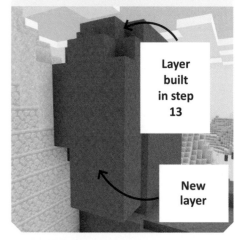

Layer built in step 13

New layer

STEP 15

Your creation should be taking shape now. This is how it should look from the front—check it out!

STEP 16

For the chest, use more **smooth red sandstone**. It will look like two connected semicircles.

STEP 17

Add **smooth red sandstone stairs** for a great way to give the chest a more realistic curved shape.

STEP 18

Below the chest shape, use the same technique and some more **smooth red sandstone** to create the stomach muscles.

STEP 19

Use smooth red sandstone for the hands resting on the lap. Make the hands two blocks high.

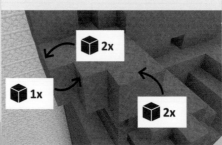

 2x

1x

2x

STEP 20

Then, use **smooth red sandstone blocks** and **smooth red sandstone slabs** to form the shape below.

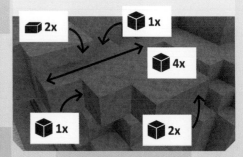

 2x

1x

4x

1x

2x

STEP 21

Use **red sandstone blocks** for the base of the beard, starting at the top of the shoulders. Copy the shape as shown, below.

STEP 22

Build the outline of the face using **smooth red sandstone**, like this. It might look complicated, but here are all the measurements you need, below.

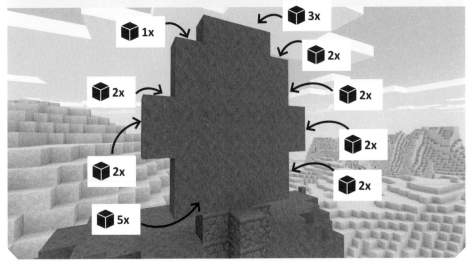

STEP 23

Remove two blocks for each eye with a one-block gap between them. Add **smooth red sandstone slabs** for eyebrows and a row of **smooth red sandstone stairs** for a nose. Use **smooth red sandstone** for a mouth, and **smooth red sandstone stairs** for the lips and the top of the beard.

STEP 24

For the headdress, simply use **red sandstone** across the top two rows. Then, use more to fill in the other gaps until it looks like this!

STEP 25

Keep hold of your **smooth red sandstone** to add a layer to the base of the shoulders from the back.

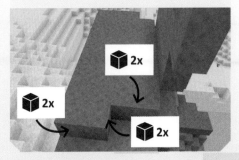

STEP 26

Then, add two **smooth red sandstone** blocks, like this. Do this on both sides.

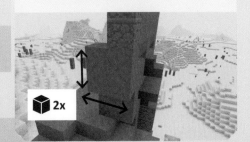

STEP 27

Use the measurements below to help you fill in each side of the head with **red sandstone**.

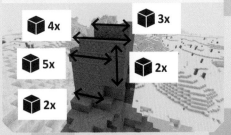

STEP 28

When both sides of the head are filled in, you can fill in the back of the head, so that it looks like this.

STEP 29

Add more rows of **red sandstone** blocks on each side of the face.

STEP 30

To add more to the shape you built in Step 29, use **red sandstone stairs** along the edges.

STEP 31

On top of the head, add a section of **red sandstone blocks**. Make it five blocks wide, four blocks high, and four blocks deep.

STEP 32

For the center of the headdress, use **smooth red sandstone** and **smooth red sandstone stairs**.

STEP 33

Build three more statues. Use **chiseled red sandstone** to build a wall across the back that's four blocks higher than the top of the statues.

STEP 34

Then, use **chiseled red sandstone** to make sloping sides, like this.

STEP 35

Next, add a row of **chiseled red sandstone** blocks across the front. This should be five blocks deep and two blocks high.

STEP 36

Use **red sandstone fencing** along the length of the first ledge. Follow that with a line of **red sandstone slabs** on both sides. Add stairs by layering **red sandstone stairs**. Now create borders to the stairs using **red sandstone fencing**. Use **red sandstone slabs** to border the rest of your walkway.

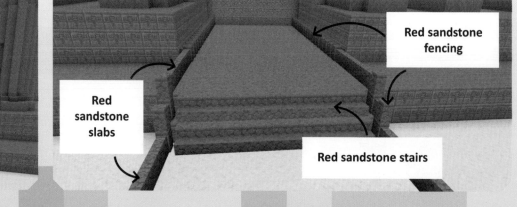

Red sandstone fencing

Red sandstone slabs

Red sandstone stairs

STEP 37

To make the smaller statues, add **armor stands** with **leather armor**. See below for where to place them.

STEP 38

At the front of the build, knock out a door right in the middle. Make it 11 blocks high and five blocks wide.

STEP 39

Then, add three rows of **chiseled red sandstone** above the door for some extra Egyptian detail.

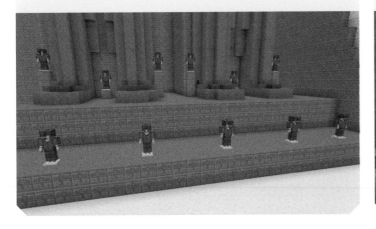

STEP 40

Above the door, knock out a rectangle that's one block deep, two blocks wide, and eight high.

STEP 41

Create this mini statue in the rectangle by using **red sandstone** and **red sandstone stairs**.

ANCIENT GREECE

With marble temples, open-air theaters and sculptures made of bronze and gold, Ancient Greece was built for the gods.

Lighthouse of Alexandria

This impressive structure is the Lighthouse of Alexandria, or the Pharos of Alexandria. It was built on an island named Pharos around 280 BCE. It's believed that it was more than 350 feet (107 meters) high, making it one of the tallest structures in the world at the time. The structure had a square base, octagonal middle section, and a cylindrical top. Sadly, the lighthouse was ruined by earthquakes, but it remains one of the most famous lighthouses in history.

Colossus of Rhodes

Take a look at this striking statue of the Greek sun god, Helios. Known as the Colossus of Rhodes, the bronze statue stood in a busy harbor and was designed by Chares of Lindos. It was built in 280 BC on the Greek island of Rhodes, and it took 12 years to complete! Sadly, the 108-foot (33-meter) tall masterpiece was destroyed in 226 BC by an earthquake.

! DID YOU KNOW?

The Colossus of Rhodes was one of the tallest statues of the ancient world.

Parthenon

This marble temple is the Parthenon and it was dedicated to Athena, the goddess of wisdom. The large structure is 101 feet (31 meters) wide and 229 feet (70 meters) long—it needed to be big enough to house a 39-foot (12-meter) high statue of Athena in gold and ivory!

Temple of Zeus

The temple was dedicated to Zeus, the god of the sky and thunder in Greek mythology. Although earthquakes have destroyed a lot of this temple, you can still get an idea of its grand scale by the size of the remaining columns. It was built in Olympia, which was where the original Olympic Games took place. The games were part of a festival that celebrated Zeus.

Odeon of Herodes Atticus

This open-air theater is found at the base of Athens' Acropolis (which means "high city"). The stone structure was badly damaged during an invasion, but that didn't keep it from being used for events and shows. It has since been rebuilt and restored. This venue seats about 5,000 people, and it's used for festivals, ballets, and plays performed on its historic stage.

PARTHENON

The Parthenon is one of Greece's most spectacular sites!
Are you ready to tackle this epic build? Let's do this!

MATERIALS

STEP 1

Start by building a rectangle of **smooth quartz blocks**. Make it 51 blocks long and 24 blocks wide. It should look like this.

51x

24x

STEP 2

Add a row of **quartz pillar blocks** around the edge of the rectangle. Leave a gap the size of one block between each one.

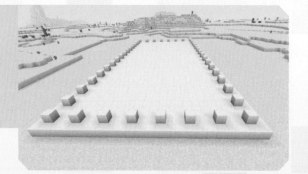

STEP 3

Add another row of **quartz pillar blocks** to each end of the rectangle, like this. Then, create the shape of the rooms using **quartz brick blocks**. This is how your build should look, seen from above.

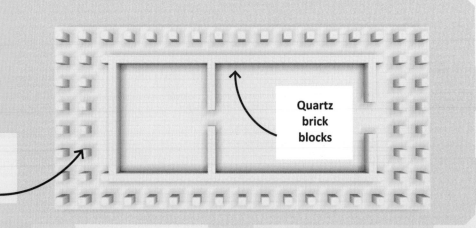

Quartz brick blocks

New rows of quartz pillar blocks

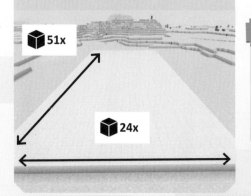

STEP 4

Now use **quartz pillar blocks** to build up the pillars and **quartz bricks** to build up the walls. When it's finished, your temple will really start to take shape.

STEP 5

When your pillars and walls are all equal height, use more **smooth quartz blocks** to build a flat roof. This will connect all parts of the Parthenon.

STEP 6

Add a row of **smooth quartz stairs** all the way along the base of your build.

STEP 8

Add a layer of **quartz bricks** to the roof of the Parthenon.

STEP 7

Then, add these **smooth quartz stairs** around the top of each pillar, too. These details will make all the difference to the look of your build.

STEP 9

To build up the pointed shape of the roof, simply use **smooth quartz blocks**. Then, use **smooth quartz stairs** to create the steplike edges.

Steplike edges

STEP 10

Along the top of the roof, add a layer of **smooth quartz stairs**. Overlap these blocks so that they stick out at the front. Do this all the way along the top of this section.

Add a layer quartz stairs that stick out here.

STEP 11

Now it's time to complete the rest of the roof. Use smooth **quartz stairs** to build it up in layers, like this, so that the roof comes to a peak at the top.

STEP 12

Take your Parthenon to the next level by adding some all-important details. Begin by placing some **armor stands** along the front, like this.

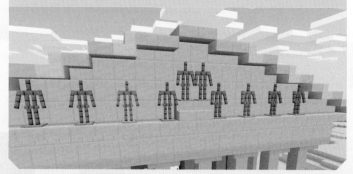

STEP 13

For the finishing touch, just place on some **Iron armor**. Good job—your build is complete!

LIGHTHOUSE OF ALEXANDRIA

Time to recreate one of the most famous lighthouses in history.

MATERIALS

The lighthouse was used to guide sailors safely into the port.

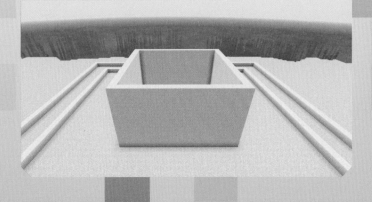

STEP 1

Use **quartz blocks** to build a square that is 51 blocks long and 51 blocks wide. Build a smaller square inside (see below), then a smaller one inside that, which is 17 blocks by 17 blocks. Add a center block in the middle square.

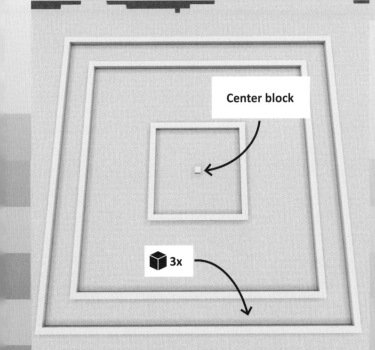

Center block

3x

STEP 2

Fill in the center square with **quartz blocks**.

STEP 3

Next, you need to build up this square. Make it 10 blocks high, and fill it in to make a solid shape.

STEP 4

Add another layer that is one block narrower all the way around. Build this one up so it is 10 blocks high, too, and fill it in. Repeat this, so that there are three blocks on top of one another, as shown.

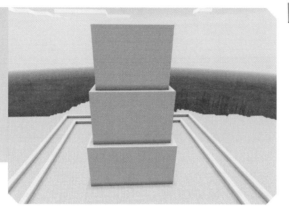

STEP 5

At the top of this, add a layer of **quartz stairs** around the edge.

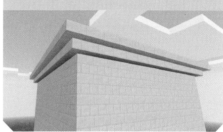

STEP 6

On the top edge, add a layer of upside-down stairs. These should face inward and have a one-block gap between each.

STEP 7

Next, create this diamond shape in the center, then fill it in with some **quartz blocks**.

STEP 8

Keep building up this diamond shape until it looks like this. It should be 10 blocks high.

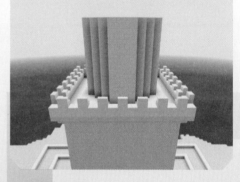

STEP 9

Inside this, add a layer of stairs around the top to create a ridge.

STEP 10

Build a square in the center that is five blocks by five blocks. Then, add four layers of blocks on top to build it up. Add a tower of blocks to each corner of the square. Each tower should be six blocks high.

STEP 11

Join up the four towers by adding a layer of six blocks on top. Then, add a square of stairs with a block on top of that.

STEP 12

Now add an **armor stand** and **iron armor** to top off the Lighthouse. Good going!

STEP 13

To make the windows, simply knock out rectangle shapes, like this. Repeat this on all four sides of your build.

STEP 14

For the door, knock out a gap at the front that is six blocks high and three blocks wide. Add a set of **quartz stairs** that is six blocks high and three blocks wide.

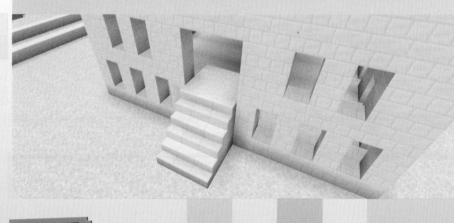

STEP 15

The Lighthouse now needs a floor. Build one so that it is at the same level as the top step you built in Step 14.

STEP 16

Fill in the area between the two biggest squares that you built back in Step 1.

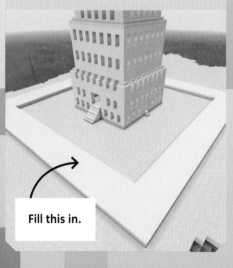

Fill this in.

STEP 17

Now build up the outside edge of this, so that it is 10 blocks high all the way around.

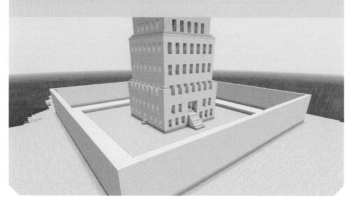

STEP 18

Add a ledge around the top edge. The ledge should be four bricks deep, just like the bottom layer!

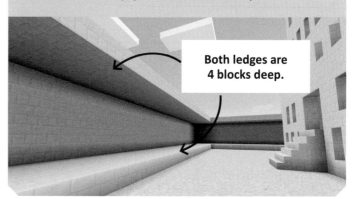

Both ledges are 4 blocks deep.

STEP 19

Then, build a square of blocks on each corner. Add **quartz stairs** on the inside top layer.

Stairs

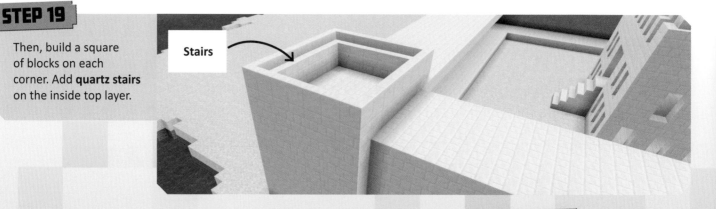

STEP 20

Find the center point at the front of your build, and make a doorway that is three blocks wide and five blocks high. Place three stairs side by side, in front of this door.

STEP 21

Add a layer of stairs around the outside edge, including the squares of blocks on each corner.

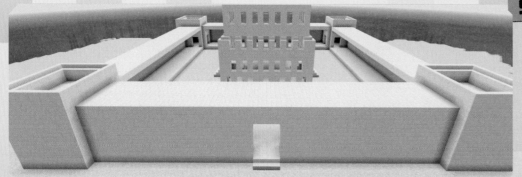

STEP 22

Use more stairs to do this all the way around the bottom edge of your build, too.

STEP 23

Create some square windows by knocking out blocks. Make the windows two blocks high and two blocks wide. Make sure you have a gap of one block between each window.

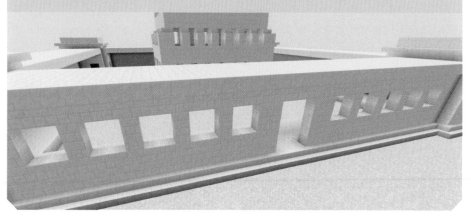

STEP 24

Knock out more blocks to make doorways for the inside corners of the corridor, like this.

STEP 25

Use **quartz pillar blocks** to create these grand pillars. Don't forget to add stairs around the tops of the pillars, too, for detail.

STEP 26

To complete your awesome build, add a layer of **stone blocks** for the flooring. Very impressive!

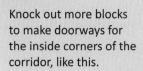

COLOSSUS OF RHODES

If you want to take things to the next level, then look no further.
It's time to recreate this imposing statue of the sun god, Helios.

MATERIALS

Our copper statue is green because when copper is exposed to the air, it reacts and changes color.

STEP 1

Build two **stone block** bases for the statue's feet to stand on. There should be a gap between them for water to flow through.

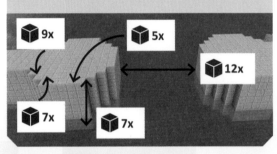

9x   5x   12x
7x   7x

STEP 2

Next, use **green concrete blocks** to create the feet. There should be one foot on each base, like this.

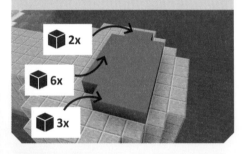

2x
6x
3x

STEP 3

On top of this, add another layer of blocks to start forming the rounded shape of the feet.

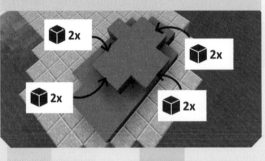

2x   2x
2x   2x

STEP 4

For ankles, add a layer that is narrower than the one below. The ankles should be a mirror image.

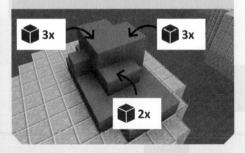

3x   3x
2x

STEP 5

Begin building the basic shape of the lower legs. Make them one block thick. Leave one row of foot blocks at the back to make the heels.

STEP 6

Now build up the legs some more. Look at the image, below, for how to angle your blocks so that the two legs will meet at the top.

STEP 7

Repeat this on the opposite leg, so that they are both leaning in toward the center.

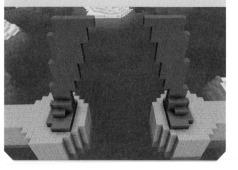

STEP 8

Give the legs some definition by adding a layer of blocks to the front side of each, as shown below.

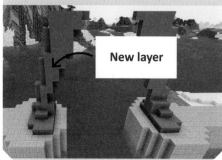

New layer

STEP 9

Add another layer of blocks to shape the top of each leg. This layer is smaller than the one in Step 8.

4x

STEP 10

Start to add layers of more **green concrete blocks** to flesh out the back of the legs, as shown.

STEP 11

Keep going until they look like this. Can you see how each new layer is a little smaller than the one before?

STEP 12

Use **lime concrete blocks** to create this shape at the top of the legs. This frame will form the bottom of the fabric the statue is wearing.

STEP 13

Now build a row of blocks upward from the edge of each leg, like this, to form the shape of his loincloth.

STEP 14

To connect the two sides and complete the frame, just add the shape shown below, on top.

STEP 15

To fill in the fabric, experiment with layering up the blocks to look like folds and creases. Use the same layering technique at the back. The fabric should look a little bit like this.

STEP 16

Keep going until you have filled in the top and bottom of the loincloth. This shows how it should look from above and below.

STEP 17

You will need more **green concrete** blocks to create this shape on top.

STEP 18

Use the same blocks to build this section up so it is four blocks high. This will be the stomach.

STEP 19

Create a small ridge at the top by adding a row of blocks at the front, like this.

STEP 20

Add a few more blocks to his stomach to look like muscles.

STEP 21

Next, build upward on both sides to create a basic torso. Your statue should be taking shape now.

3x

4x

STEP 22

Don't forget to fill in his back. It should look something like this from behind.

STEP 23

See below for how to fill in the front section. Then, add three extra blocks on each side, like this.

STEP 24

Now fill in this area the entire way around. Remember to keep the rounded shape of the torso.

STEP 25

Use more blocks to add this shape to the front, top edge. This will form the chest of your statue.

STEP 26

Fill in the shape you built in Step 25, so that it looks like the picture, below.

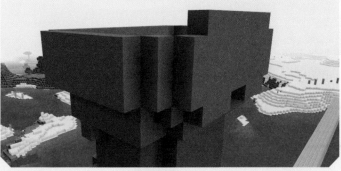

STEP 27

Add another two layers of blocks on top of this shape. Be sure you make each layer one block smaller on each level.

STEP 28

To give your build some serious muscles, add blocks as shown. It works best if you leave small gaps between them.

STEP 29

Create this shape on each side of the build. This will be the base of the two shoulders, so make sure they match.

STEP 30

The right arm needs to be raised, so try building up the shoulder. Lay three blocks across the top of the shape you built in Step 29.

3x

STEP 31

Make this curved shape for the bottom of his right arm. This should be built into the middle of the shape you made in Step 29 and Step 30.

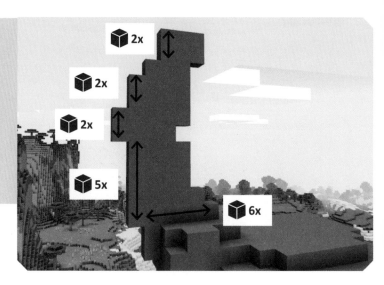

2x
2x
2x
5x
6x

STEP 32

Give the right arm some more definition! Do this to the front and back to make it rounded.

STEP 33

At the end of the arm, make this shape. This will become the hand gripping the torch.

STEP 34

Look at the image below to see how the left shoulder should look. It's ready for the second arm.

STEP 35

Make the basic arm shape, like you did in Step 31. But this time, make sure it's pointing down at his side.

STEP 36

Now make this arm rounded like his right one. Be sure to add layers to the front and back of the arm.

STEP 37

At the end of the arm, create a shape like this for the left hand at his side.

STEP 38

At the top of the torso, add some blocks for the neck. This will then become the base of the head.

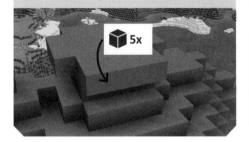

5x

STEP 39

Build up the head, and add some facial features. See below for a guide to the measurements.

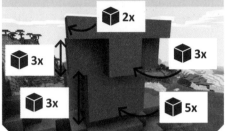

2x
3x
3x
3x
5x

STEP 40

At the top of the head, use some **lime concrete**. This will make the base of the statue's crown.

STEP 41

Layer up the **lime concrete** to create the pattern shown here.

STEP 42

Give the crown some points made from **lime concrete blocks**. The middle one should be the biggest.

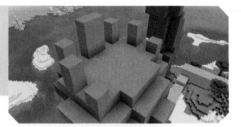

STEP 43

Use more **lime concrete blocks** to build a torch in the right hand, as shown.

STEP 44

For the finishing touch, use **dark prismarine blocks** to make a flame.

ANCIENT CHINA

Dive in and explore Ancient China. From sacred sites, to a forbidden city and the longest wall on the planet, China is full of incredible builds.

Giant Wild Goose Pagoda

This sacred Buddhist site, also known as the "Dayan Pagoda", is over 1,000 years old. The seven-story high, square-shaped monument is the city of Xi'an's most famous landmark! At 210 feet (64 meters) tall, it towers over nearby buildings, and visitors can climb it to enjoy views over the city.

Temple of Heaven

This temple was built for emperors to worship heaven. The building is round because the emperor wanted it to reflect the Ancient Chinese belief that heaven was dome-like and protected the square-shaped earth below.

Great Wall of China

The Great Wall is the longest wall in the world and the longest structure ever built by humans. The Great Wall of China is built across northern China and southern Mongolia. Stretching over 21,000 kilometers (13,000 miles), this wall was built to keep invaders out. The earliest parts of the wall are 2,000 years old!

DID YOU KNOW?

The tallest part of the wall is about 26 feet (8 meters) high.

Forbidden City

This epic palace complex in Beijing contains 980 buildings and almost 9,000 rooms, all tucked behind a city wall. It took over 1 million workers to build the Forbidden City (1406–1420). Protecting the emperors living there was vital. It was named the Forbidden City because ordinary people were not allowed inside.

This building is called the Hall of Supreme Harmony.

Yuyuan Garden

Yuyuan Garden, or "Garden of Peace and Comfort", is in the center of Shanghai's Old City. It was built more than 400 years ago by a man who wanted his elderly parents to relax in the gardens. Besides flowers and plants, the garden is full of classical Chinese architecture with archways, bridges, and sculptures.

GIANT WILD GOOSE PAGODA

Let's start with this magnificent seven-story sacred site to test your tower-building skills.

MATERIALS

STEP 1

Build a square using **stone brick blocks**— it should be 65 blocks long and 65 blocks wide. Then, build it up so it is five blocks high, and fill it in.

STEP 2

Then, add these **stone brick wall blocks** around the top, like this.

STEP 5

To make these stairs smaller, add rows of **stone brick stairs** along each one, like this.

Use more **stone brick wall blocks** at the ends of your stairs. These will form a bannister for the stairs and give them a finishing touch.

STEP 3

Find the center point at the front of your build, then make this shape using **stone brick blocks**. It should be five blocks by three blocks and three blocks high!

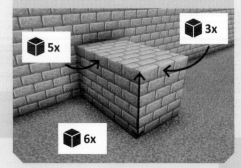

5x

3x

6x

STEP 4

Add **stone brick blocks** on both sides of what you built in Step 3 to create stairs, like this. Next, knock out the section behind it in order to create the next layer of stairs.

STEP 5

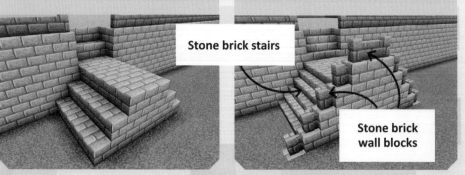

Stone brick stairs

Stone brick wall blocks

STEP 6

Grab **gray wool blocks** to build another square on top of the big square you built in Step 1. This new square should be 11 blocks in from the outer edge, and it should be eight blocks high.

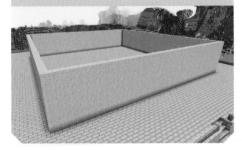

STEP 7

Add two layers of upside-down **andesite stairs** around the top edge of this square. It should now look like this.

STEP 8

Now add another layer of **andesite stairs**, but this time, flip them upright, so that they create this shape when the two layers are together.

STEP 9

Add three more layers of **andesite stairs**. Then, make these level by using **birch wood plank blocks**.

Birch wood plank blocks

STEP 10

Add another layer of the **andesite stairs** around the edges.

STEP 11

Now it's time to build up the wall, just like you did in Step 6. Again, this wall should be eight blocks high. Then, repeat Steps 7 to 10.

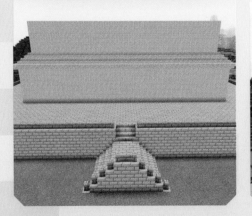

STEP 12

Repeat these steps until you have seven levels. Around the top edge, add one layer of **andesite stairs**. Make sure they are facing down.

STEP 13

Fill in the top using **gray wool blocks**, and then add six layers of **andesite blocks**. Your build should now look like this.

ANCIENT CHINA

STEP 14

To add some detail, use rows of **andesite stairs** on top of the blocks you've already put down. This will make the steps narrower.

STEP 15

Fill in the top using **andesite blocks**, then create a pillar using more **andesite blocks**. Make this pillar six blocks high and three blocks wide. Then, put **andesite stairs** on the edges and in the center. Add an **andesite block** to the top, too!

Andesite stairs

STEP 16

Use more **andesite stairs** around the top block, as shown. Then, build a pillar in the center, six blocks high, using **andesite blocks**.

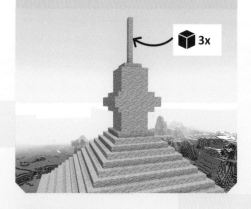

3x

STEP 17

Knock out windows down all four sides of the building. They look best when they're in a straight row down the front. For the finishing touch, use **andesite stairs** for window frames.

Andesite stairs

Experiment with different biomes to reflect the part of the world where your build is based.

GREAT WALL OF CHINA

Put your building skills to the ultimate test, and take on China's world-famous wall!

MATERIALS

STEP 1

Make sure that you have a large space to build on. The ground doesn't need to be totally flat—just avoid any lakes or water that could get in the way!

STEP 2

Grab some **stone brick blocks** to create a frame for your wall. It should be around eight blocks wide. You can make it a little crooked, like this!

STEP 3

Next, use **stone brick blocks** to build up a section of your wall, like this. Keep going until it is four blocks high.

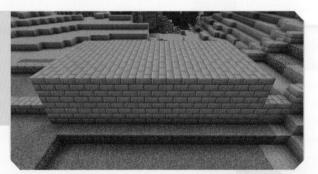

It works best if your frame follows the curves and shapes of the landscape.

STEP 4

Now you need to add another three layers using the same blocks. These layers should be six blocks wide (instead of eight).

STEP 5

Add a row of **stone brick stairs**, like this. This should then stick out to create a ledge.

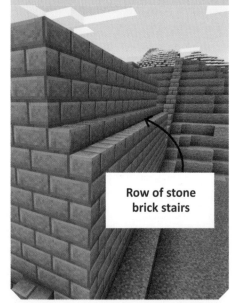

Row of stone brick stairs

STEP 6

Next, add two rows of **stone brick blocks**, so that they run along the top edges of the wall. This will create a pathway along the wall.

STEP 7

Use **stone brick stairs** along the top edges. These should face inward, and there should be a gap between each one.

STEP 9

This is how your build will look as it goes down a hill. Can you see how it follows the natural shape?

STEP 8

Repeat this process along large stretches of your wall. Remember to follow the shape of your landscape, so that the wall goes up and down.

STEP 10

When going downhill, lay out your **stone brick blocks** to create steps. Add four **stone brick stairs** to each layer of blocks. These images show how it should look from above.

STEP 11

If there are any big dips along your wall, you can try this technique. By adding in stairs, the wall can follow the rise and fall of the hills.

STEP 12

Give your wall some character by adding in some texture and replacing blocks with **cracked stone brick blocks** and **mossy stone bricks**.

STEP 13

At the end of your wall, create a square of **brick stone blocks** to make your guard tower. This should be 14 blocks by 14 blocks.

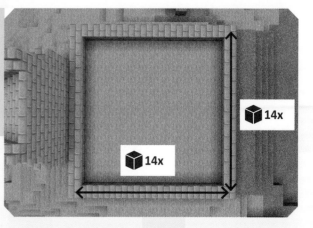

14x

14x

STEP 14

Fill in the guard tower, so that it is level with your wall, like this!

STEP 15

Around the edge of the guard tower, add a layer of **stone brick stairs**. This will form an edging.

STEP 16

Then, in each corner, build a pillar that is five blocks high. Connect these four pillars by adding a layer of blocks for a roof, like this.

STEP 17

Add **stone brick stairs** along the top edge. They work best if you leave a gap between each one. Make sure these are facing inward, too.

STEP 18

Now fill in the walls of the tower. Start with the left and right sides, and then move on to the side leading to your main wall. On the main wall side, knock out a door and windows. The back can be left open.

STEP 19

Next, knock out some windows on each side of the tower to let some light flood in.

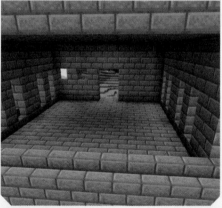

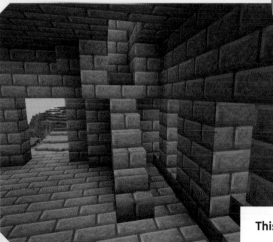

STEP 20

Create a small staircase from **stone brick stairs**. This should lead straight up to the roof of your tower.

STEP 21

Follow the staircase all the way to the top. Create this shape at the top of the tower.

Leave a little gap, like this.

This is the exit from the stairs.

STEP 22

Build up this shape so it's three blocks high, but leave the gap since this will make the doorway. Then, add these points on each end for the roof.

Points at each end

STEP 23

To fill in the roof, use stone brick stairs. This will help to create the sloped edge.

STEP 24

Your wall is really starting to take shape. Now all you need to do is continue this process from the other side of your tower until it is all filled in.

FORBIDDEN CITY

Beijing's Forbidden City is a huge palace complex. It would take years to build every building contained inside, so we're focusing on just one for now.

MATERIALS

STEP 1

First, lay a base of **smooth stone blocks**. It should be 92 blocks wide and 56 blocks long. Make sure it's two blocks high, as shown below.

STEP 2

On top of the base, add two more layers. Make the first 86 by 50 blocks and the next 80 by 44 blocks—each of these layers needs to be two blocks high.

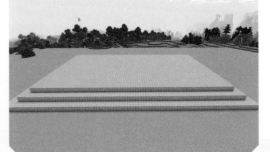

The Forbidden City was home to various Chinese Emperors and their families.

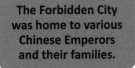

STEP 3

For the entrance stairs, start by adding markers. To do this, knock out a block on each layer that is 14 blocks from the end, like this. There will be a gap of three blocks between each, as shown.

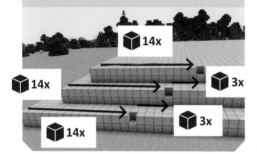

STEP 4

Use the markers on the bottom layer as a guide to building a new section from the same blocks. This area should also be two blocks high.

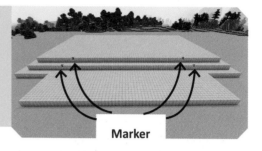

Marker

STEP 5

Use the markers to add the next two layers, like this, so that you have three even layers. This will create big block stairs all the way around.

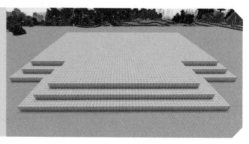

STEP 6

On the big base area, add one layer of **smooth stone blocks**. It should be six blocks from the outer edges and three blocks in from the front and back. Build a row of **red concrete blocks** on the left and right edges—make sure these are one block in from the edges.

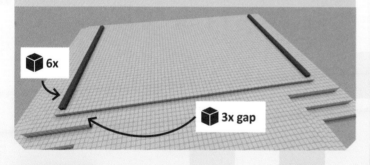

STEP 7

Now, use **red concrete blocks** to mark where your pillars will go along the rows you built in Step 6. Check out our measurements below to help you!

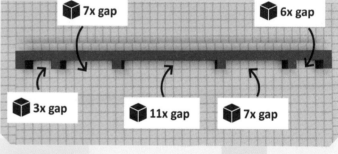

STEP 8

Mark out pillars at the front and back. Have a one-block gap at each end and a five-block gap between the next three pillars. There should be an eigh-block gap in the middle. Now, do the same from the other side.

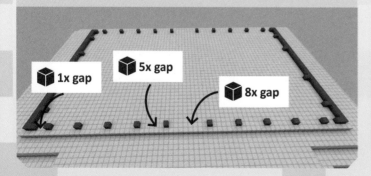

STEP 9

From the second marker (Step 7), build across 17 blocks, then leave a gap of three. Next, add three, leave a gap of three, then add three more. Do the same on the other side so there is a gap of six in the middle.

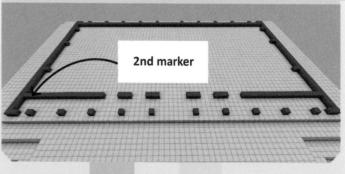

2nd marker

STEP 10

Build up all of the **red concrete blocks** by 10, until it looks like this. This is where things will start to take shape.

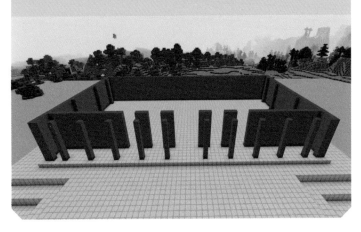

STEP 11

Inside the red walls, add a layer of **white terracotta blocks** to create the floor.

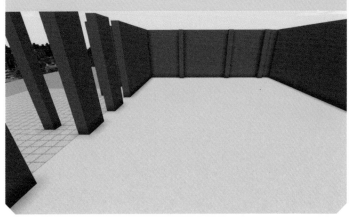

STEP 12

Build up the front so that it looks like this. Leave space for the doors, as shown below.

This is the view from inside.

STEP 13

Add another layer of pillars directly in front of this. These should line up with the existing pillars at the front.

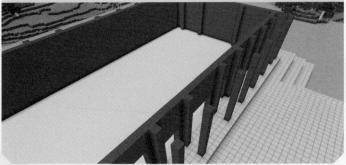

STEP 14

Use the existing pillars to mark out where the rest will go, like this. Use the same spacing as you did in Step 8 to help get this right.

STEP 15

When you're happy with your pillar positions, you can build them all up by 10 blocks.

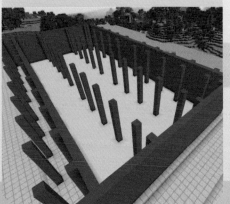

STEP 16

Add a layer of **glazed orange terracotta blocks** that is two blocks high to the top.

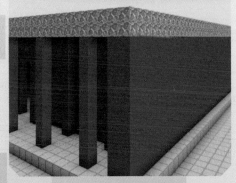

STEP 17

Keep hold of the **glazed orange terracotta blocks** because they're perfect for decorating the top of the pillars across the front of your build.

STEP 18

Use **jungle planks blocks** to build this shape on top. The structure should start four blocks in from each edge and be three blocks high.

STEP 19

With the same blocks, create these shapes in each corner. Don't forget to check out our labels below to get it right.

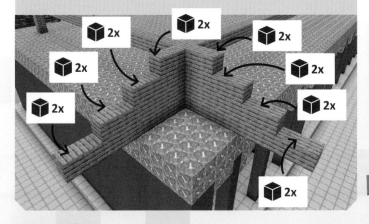

STEP 20

Fill in the top using more **jungle planks blocks** until it looks like this from above.

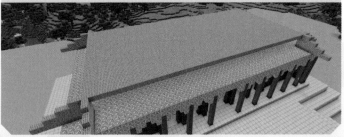

STEP 21

Fill in the sides using the blocks placed in Step 19 to guide you. You should get an awesome effect.

STEP 22

To complete the structure, fill in the corners so there are no gaps, as shown here.

STEP 23

Then, you can add **jungle planks stairs** to each layer, like this. These details create a really authentic look.

STEP 24

Now add two layers of **glazed orange terracotta blocks** on top, so that it looks like the image below.

STEP 25

On top of this, create a new frame like you did in Step 18. But this one should be two blocks away from the edges, as shown.

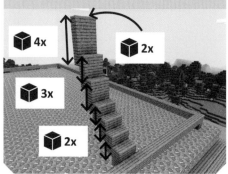

STEP 26

Find the center point on each of the shorter sides of the frame. Then, copy the shape and dimensions in the image below.

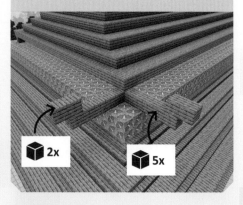

STEP 27

Repeat this on the opposite side of the frame, so that you can connect the two sides, like this.

STEP 28

Use this frame to fill in a roof from **jungle planks blocks**. Then, add **jungle planks stairs** to each edge.

STEP 29

Next, you need to create this shape in each corner, so that it juts out to create a ledge.

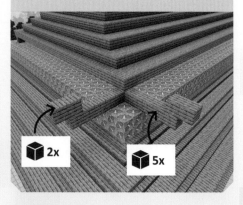

STEP 30

Use the blocks in Step 29 to help you to fill in the ledge all the way around.

STEP 31

Go back and add more layers of **jungle planks stairs** to the top.

STEP 32

Use upside-down **jungle planks stairs** to the underside of every roof ledge so it looks like this.

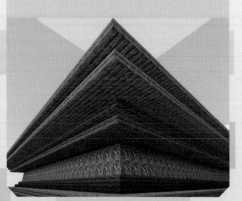

STEP 33

Build layers of **polished andesite stairs** at the front. Make the center stairs line up with the door at the main entrance. Put the other stairs eight blocks from the center stairs.

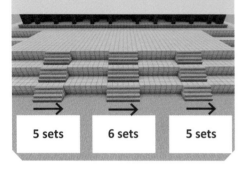

| 5 sets | 6 sets | 5 sets |

STEP 34

Next, add rows of **polished andesite stairs** in front of the red pillars. See below for how to line them up. Also add **stone brick wall blocks** to the top of all your **smooth stone block** edges.

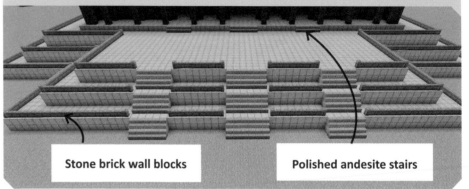

Stone brick wall blocks

Polished andesite stairs

STEP 35

Let the light into your build by knocking out some windows. Their shape should reflect the shape of the glazed orange terracotta blocks.

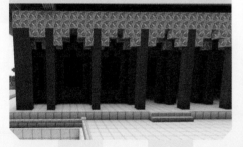

STEP 36

Now it's time to move inside. Hang **lanterns** from the ceiling, and add some to the pillars, too.

STEP 37

Finally, check out how effective these **crimson fences** are when you add them to the windows.

ANCIENT AMERICAS

From colossal carvings to cliffs in the clouds, let's take a trip to this ancient civilization.

Pyramid of the Sun

This is the largest pyramid in Teotihuacán, which is an ancient city in Mexico. The Pyramid of the Sun stands 216 feet (66 meters) above ground level, and on one side of the pyramid are 248 steps leading straight to the top. In the 1970s, explorers found caves and chambers connected by tunnels underneath the pyramid.

Machu Picchu

Machu Picchu was built in the fifteenth century during the Inca Empire. Today, people travel from all over the world to experience the incredible sight. Machu Picchu is built into the dramatic mountain and valley landscape of southern Peru. It is made up of huge walls and ramps, along with many religious and agricultural structures.

! DID YOU KNOW?

Earthquakes are common here. The buildings don't use mortar, so the stones move around safely during these tremors without being destroyed.

Cliff Palace at Mesa Verde

Mesa Verde was home to the Pueblo people who lived in villages built into the sides of cliffs. This is the Cliff Palace and North America's biggest cliff dwelling. In the 1200s, about 100 people would have lived here, and it had 150 rooms. Families shared rooms, which they got to by climbing wooden ladders.

Copán

The ruins of an ancient city named Copán are a key site of the Maya civilization. The 250-acre (100-hectare) site in Honduras has the remains of temples, pyramids, and steps. Leading up to one of the temples is the Hieroglyphic Stairway, which is carved with symbols.

Olmec Stone Heads

These colossal stone heads were carved by the Olmec, who had an ancient civilization in Mexico. Many stone-carved artifacts were discovered from this period, but the 17 stone heads are the most famous of them all. It is believed that they are portraits of Olmec rulers. The stone heads can be as tall as 11 feet (3.4 meters)!

OLMEC STONE HEAD

These ancient stone heads were originally carved from basalt boulders.
Luckily, your material is a little easier to build with!

MATERIALS

You could add vines to
your Olmec stone head.

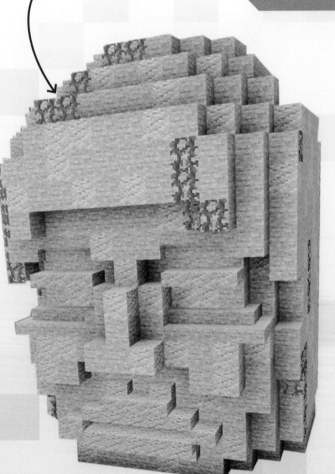

STEP 1

Make a cross from **stone blocks**
that is 17 blocks high and 13
wide. The 13-block row should
be 12 blocks from the bottom.

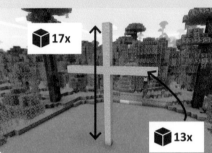

17x

13x

STEP 2

Use **stone blocks** to join up the
ends of the 13-block row that
you built in Step 1. This will form
a circle, as shown.

STEP 3

Next, make an arch across the top of the cross. This will
become the forehead. Grab plenty of **stone blocks**, then
fill in its forehead, like this.

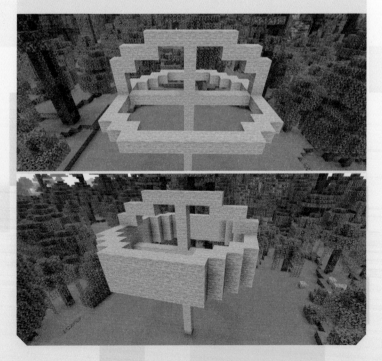

STEP 4

Fill in the top of the head using layers of blocks that get smaller toward the top. This will make it appear curved.

STEP 5

Fill in each side of the Olmec stone head using the Step 4 technique.

STEP 6

Move on to the back of the head. This section needs filling in, too.

STEP 7

Add **stone stairs** behind the top of the forehead—this layer will help to create depth. Lay a straight line of **stone blocks** across the bottom to mark out the edge of the face.

Mark out the bottom of its face.

STEP 8

It's time to give the build some character. Start by filling in the face and nose areas.

STEP 9

Use **stone slabs** to form the eyebrows. This helps to define the face and give it character.

STEP 10

Begin to build up the nose with more layers to create depth.

STEP 11

For the cheeks, add some rows of **stone stairs**, like this!

Use **cobblestone slabs** for the eyes, and follow this picture to show you the shape.

STEP 12

Try shaping the bottom of the cheeks, as shown here.

STEP 13

Form the mouth out of **cobblestone** and **cobblestone stairs**.

STEP 15

You could try taking out the blocks on the top corners of your build. This should create a more rounded head shape.

STEP 16

Then, use this same technique along the bottom edge. You should see how it softens the edges so they appear more curved.

STEP 17

To take your masterpiece further, replace random blocks with **cobblestone blocks**. This will create a realistic texture!

PYRAMID OF THE SUN

It took thousands of people to create this pyramid. Let's see if you can take it on solo!

STEP 1

This build is pretty epic and takes up a lot of room! You'll need to clear a big, flat space before you begin.

STEP 2

Use **light gray terracotta blocks** to create a square that is 126 blocks long and 126 blocks wide.

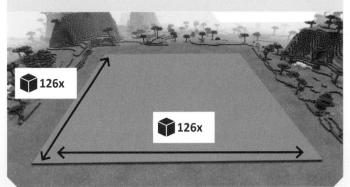

126x

126x

MATERIALS

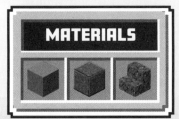

It's believed that there would have been an altar at the top of the pyramid.

DID YOU KNOW?

One of the materials used to build the Pyramid of the Sun was red volcanic rock.

ANCIENT AMERICAS

DIFFICULTY: INTERMEDIATE   BUILD TIME: 2+ HOURS

STEP 3

Build up 10 layers of blocks on top of this square. Each new layer should be one block smaller than the one below, like this.

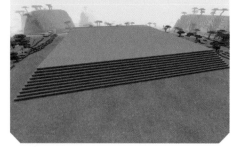

STEP 4

Now build three blocks in from the edge. Add another 10 layers of blocks going in one block at a time—just like in Step 3.

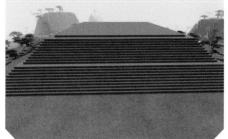

STEP 5

Build three blocks in from the edge like you did in Step 4. Then, build six more layers that go in one block at a time.

STEP 6

Begin building three blocks in from the edge, and add one more layer, like the picture below.

STEP 7

On top of this, add another layer with an overhang. This means that it will stick out over the edge of the layer below.

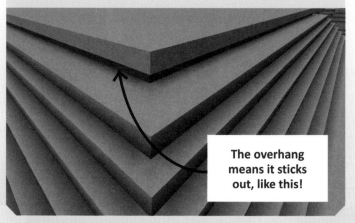

The overhang means it sticks out, like this!

STEP 8

Now build four more layers on top of this. Each layer should go in one block at a time.

STEP 9

Use the same blocks to build a shape like this on the top of everything you have built so far.

STEP 10

Fill in the shape completely. Then, build a smaller version of the same shape on top, as shown in the picture.

STEP 11

Fill in this shape, too. The top of your build should now look like this.

STEP 12

Using the same blocks, make this diamond shape on top of your build. Start from the middle, and work your way out to make sure it is central.

STEP 13

Check out your pyramid from the front. Use two blocks to make a marker for the center point at the base of the pyramid on the bottom layer.

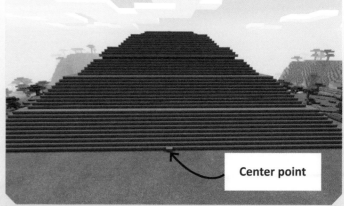

Center point

STEP 14

Add more blocks to this marker, so that it is 12 blocks deep and 30 blocks wide. It should be two blocks high.

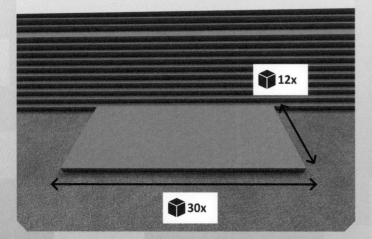

 12x

30x

STEP 15

Next, add two more layers to create steps, like this. Each layer should also be two blocks high—just as in Step 14.

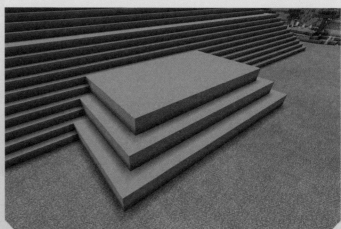

STEP 16

On top of this, add a chunky step. This last step should be three blocks deep and three blocks high.

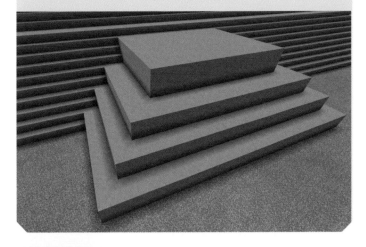

STEP 17

Now, move four blocks away from the center step. Here, add two sets of **granite stairs** side by side.

STEP 18

Then, add one **granite block** on either side of the **granite stairs**.

STEP 19

Repeat this so that there are 10 layers of **granite stairs** going up the front of the pyramid, diagonally.

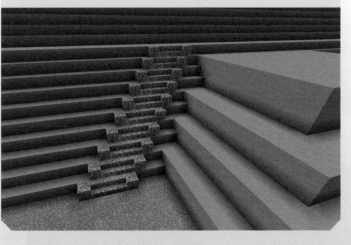

STEP 20

Now repeat Step 19 until both sets of steps match the middle of the blocks at the front of the pyramid.

STEP 21

At the top of the steps, add **granite stairs**. Make these as wide as the big steps. Add one **granite block** on each side.

STEP 22

Repeat this to build 10 layers of stairs that go all the way up this section, like this.

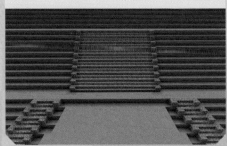

STEP 23

Then, add a single block of **granite stairs** with a **single granite block** on either side. Use the picture below to help you with the placing.

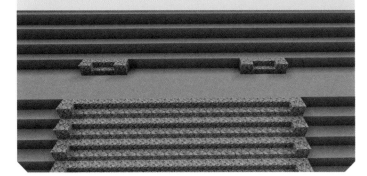

STEP 24

Repeat this until there are six layers of stairs. You should have two flights of steps up to the next section.

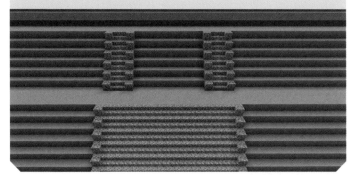

STEP 25

Moving up to the next section, knock out a row of center blocks. This knocked-out section should be 11 blocks high.

STEP 26

Finally, fill in this hollow section with more granite steps. Your build should now be complete.

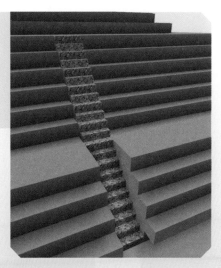

MACHU PICCHU

There are few more iconic places than southern Peru's Machu Picchu.
Can you build an amazing replica?

MATERIALS

Machu Picchu is Peru's most popular tourist destination.

STEP 1

First, you need to find a wide, open space. You could either search for a natural empty space, or choose a space and terraform it.

STEP 2

Use **dirt blocks** to build a wall. It can be as wide as your natural space allows—ours is 20 blocks wide, three blocks deep, and six blocks high.

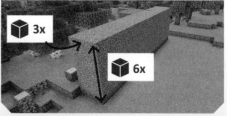

 3x

6x

STEP 3

Now add another layer that is four blocks high and two blocks deep.

STEP 4

Add another layer that is two blocks high and two blocks deep—like steps. Lay grass across the top of each layer.

STEP 5

Cover the front of each step using **cobblestone blocks**. It should look like this when you've finished this step.

STEP 6

Use the **dirt blocks** again to build more walls, as shown below.

STEP 7

Use the layering technique from Step 3 to create steps here, too.

STEP 8

Again, cover the tops of the steps with grass, as in Step 4.

STEP 9

Then, add more **cobblestone blocks** to the front of each level.

STEP 10

At the ends of your walls, use **dirt blocks** to create this curved shape.

STEP 11

Lay grass across the top of these corner blocks to match the rest.

STEP 12

Next, use **grass blocks** to build a platform that is one block high. Try and make it look like a natural or organic shape.

STEP 13

Inside this shape, add another platform that is slightly smaller. This time, make it two blocks high on top.

STEP 14

Make sure you line all of the edges with **cobblestone blocks**, as shown in the picture below.

STEP 15

Now, build smaller platforms using **grass blocks**. Line these with **cobblestone blocks**, too.

STEP 16

On the far left platform, use **cobblestone blocks** to create this shape. Look at how it builds up to a point, like a roof.

STEP 17

Repeat this at the opposite end, and then join the two together using the same blocks.

STEP 18

Next to this structure, use the same blocks to create this shape. Make sure it has gaps in the sides, like this.

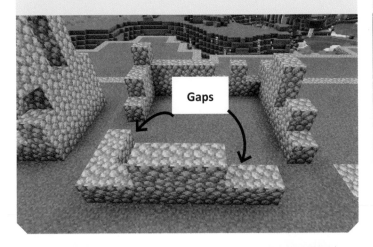

Gaps

STEP 19

To the right of this, add a third shape. Your basic structure should now look like this! Use stairs to create more detail.

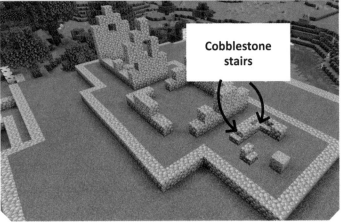

Cobblestone stairs

STEP 20

Add **cobblestone blocks** to create these structures in between your smaller platforms.

STEP 21

On one of the small platforms, build a structure like this one.

STEP 22

Between the small platforms, lay out lines, like this.

STEP 23

For more detailed staircases, try adding layered **cobblestone stairs**.

STEP 24

Use **cobblestone blocks** to create ledges coming off the platforms.

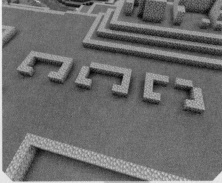

STEP 25

Now add **cobblestone stairs** to these ledges so they look like this.

STEP 26

To add some detail, add sets of **cobblestone stairs** on top of each other.

STEP 27

The picture below shows you how you can create effects by adding more **cobblestone stairs**.

STEP 28

Single sets of **cobblestone stairs** work well in corners. Awesome!

STEP 29

Try adding more structures, like this one, to fill in any big gaps on your platforms.

STEP 30

Your build should be starting to take shape now. This is how it could look from a distance.

STEP 31

Next, go to the wall you created in Step 9. Replace these blocks with **stone blocks** and **mossy cobblestone blocks**.

Mossy cobblestone blocks

Stone blocks

STEP 32

Use **grass blocks** to build up a frame that reaches outward. This should be about 10 blocks high.

STEP 33

You will need plenty of blocks for this next step. Use them to fill in the big frame you have just created.

STEP 34

Take a good look at this picture to help you see how your corners should look.

STEP 35

Now add sets of **cobblestone stairs** to the corners.

STEP 36

Last but not least, use your shovel to create walkways by removing areas of unwanted grass, like this.

GREAT PYRAMID AND SPHINX

You couldn't build the ancient wonders of the world without including these ultimate Egyptian structures.

The Great Pyramid of Giza

Not far from the Great Sphinx are the pyramids of Giza—tombs built 4,500 years ago. Millions of stone blocks were used in their construction, and it is believed that they weighed as much as 15 tons!

The Great Sphinx of Giza

Meet one of Egypt's most famous landmarks. The Sphinx of Giza is a 240-foot (73-meter) long statue made from limestone. The mythical creature sits on the banks of the Nile in Giza, Egypt. Its human face is probably based on Pharaoh Khafre, as it is thought to have been built during his reign.

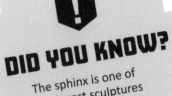

DID YOU KNOW?

The sphinx is one of the biggest sculptures in the world!

Are you ready to build these epic Egyptian creations? Here we go ...

MATERIALS

STEP 1

Using **smooth sandstone**, build a square base that is 31 blocks by 31 blocks.

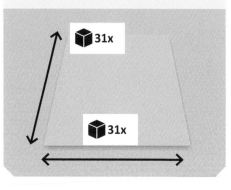

31x

31x

STEP 2

Build up the pyramid, so that it gets gradually smaller each level up you go. There are 16 levels to this one.

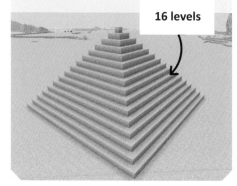

16 levels

STEP 3

Nearby, make a second pyramid with a base that is 61 blocks by 61 blocks. This pyramid will be 32 layers high.

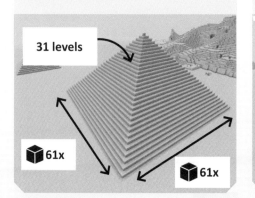

31 levels

61x

61x

STEP 4

Then, build another pyramid along from this, with a base of 71 blocks by 71 blocks. This one will be 36 layers high.

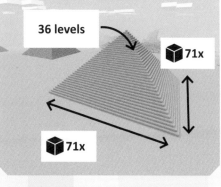

36 levels

71x

71x

STEP 5

In front of your pyramids, build a big cube and big rectangle for sphinx torso, like this.

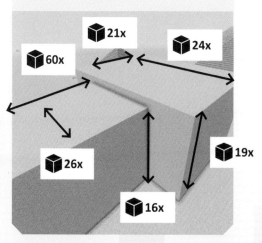

21x

60x

24x

26x

19x

16x

STEP 6

At the front of the cube, add 10 blocks sticking out, as shown. Add three blocks to each side.

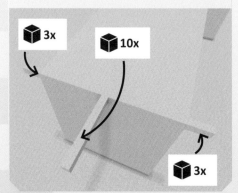

3x

10x

3x

STEP 7

Now use these to start creating a curved frame, as shown below.

STEP 8

From this frame, build down to the ground so it looks like this!

STEP 9

Sticking out at the front of this, add an outline of the legs. Each leg should be 41 blocks long and 9 blocks wide.

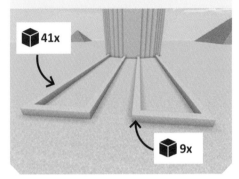

41x

9x

STEP 10

Down the middle of each leg, build a frame that is five blocks high. It should reach the whole way along the leg outline.

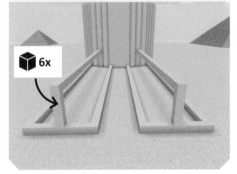

6x

STEP 11

For the back legs, build this frame where the cube and rectangle connect. Do this on both sides.

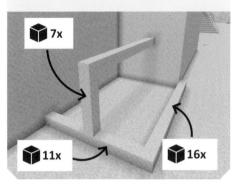

7x

11x

16x

STEP 12

When you're happy with the frames, you can start to fill in the front and back legs.

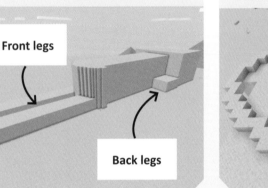

Front legs

Back legs

STEP 13

At the top of the torso (near the front), build this shape using the same blocks.

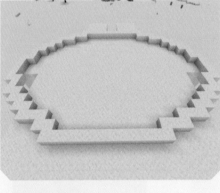

STEP 14

Now build up the four corners of the shape you built in Step 13.

STEP 15

Use these corners to help you fill in this area. Then, add two more layers that get smaller each time.

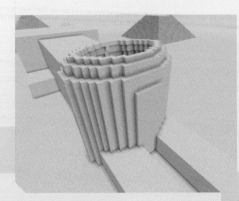

STEP 16

Next, build this shape around the bottom edge of the front leg. Repeat on the other side.

STEP 17

Behind this, add a row of blocks that curve in toward the torso.

STEP 18

Build up a frame, like this, from the joint. This will be the upper leg.

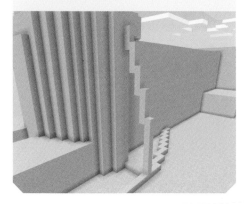

STEP 19

Use blocks to join up the top of the torso to the top of the leg frame.

Build down.

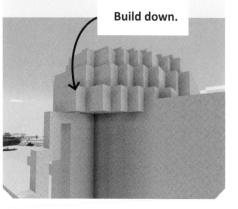

STEP 20

Use the frame to build the back of the leg by filling in the space.

Build across this way.

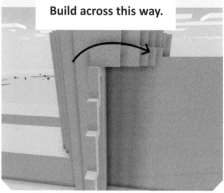

STEP 21

Fill in any gaps in the top of the leg, as shown below.

Gap

Filled in

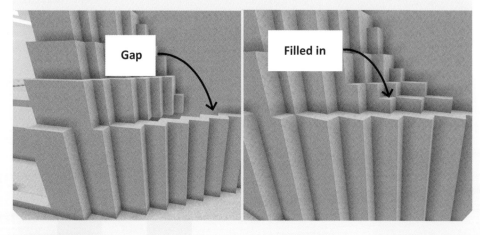

STEP 22

Next, build these rows of blocks along the front of the legs.

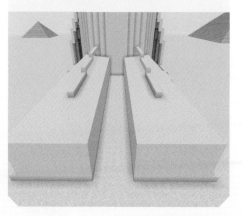

STEP 23

To create a curved leg shape, start to knock away blocks along the front inside of the legs, like this.

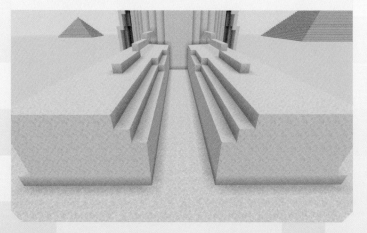

STEP 24

Then, begin knocking away these blocks on the outside edge of the front legs.

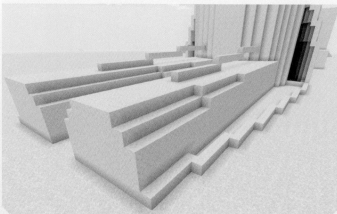

STEP 25

Now, move on to the back legs. Keep knocking out blocks along the back outside edges, so that they look like this.

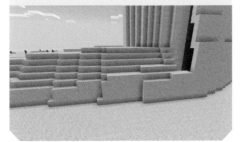

STEP 26
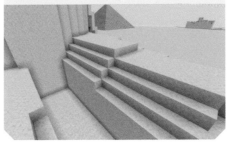

Use the same technique for shaping the inside edges of the back legs.

STEP 27

This is how your build should now look from above.

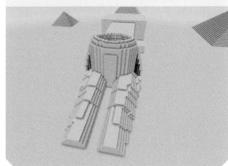

STEP 28

It's important to take time to go back and fill in any gaps you might have missed.

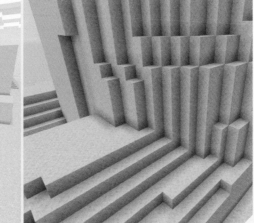

STEP 29

Shape the torso by knocking away blocks near the back legs on both sides of the sphinx.

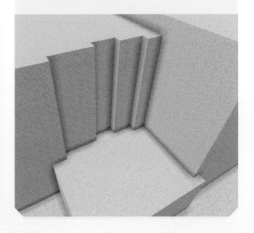

STEP 30

Along the side of the torso, knock out this shape.

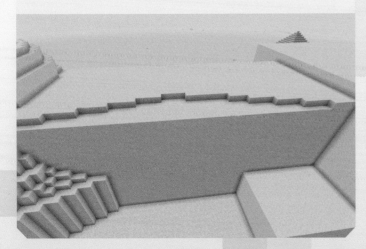

STEP 31

Keep removing blocks downward in layers, like steps. Repeat this on the other side, so they match.

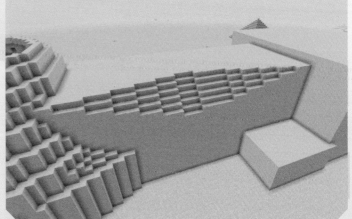

STEP 32

Create this shape coming out from the back of the neck. Make sure it is wide at the base with a pointed end.

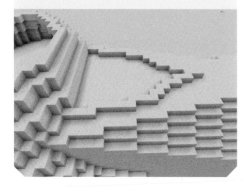

STEP 33

Build up this shape until it is six layers high. Remember that it should get smaller each time, as shown below.

STEP 34

At the back of the torso, add a layer of blocks blocks that look a little like a semicircle.

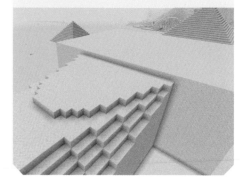

STEP 35

Add another layer of blocks on top of this. Extend this new layer all the way across the back of your sphinx, so it looks like the image.

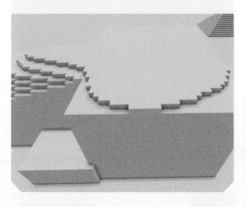

STEP 36

Try this technique to round off each corner of the back section. This should help make your sphinx look more realistic.

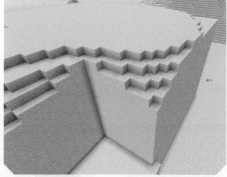

STEP 37

Look at the picture to see how to build a frame down the side edge. This is where the back leg will go.

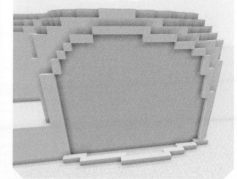

STEP 38

Look at the picture to see how to build a frame down the side edge. This is where the back leg will go.

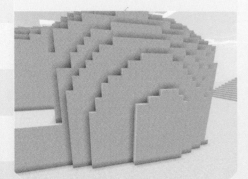

STEP 39

At the back of the sphinx, use the same layering technique to create a curved shape, as shown below.

STEP 40

Add a row of blocks to bridge the gap above the flat shape of the back legs.

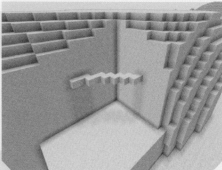

STEP 41

Use this bridge (Step 40) to help you fill in this area between the torso and the leg.

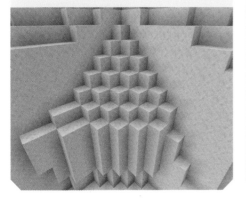

STEP 42

Knock away the edges of the back legs to form a softer shape.

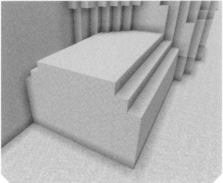

STEP 43

Next, add these blocks at the end of the leg to make toes.

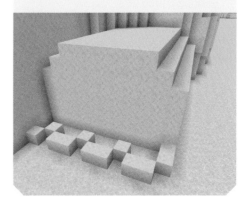

STEP 44

Build up the toes using **smooth sandstone blocks** and **smooth sandstone stairs.**

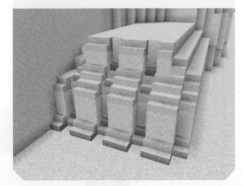

STEP 45

When you've done this on both back legs, make the shapes below for the toes on the front legs.

STEP 46

Again, build up the front toes using **smooth sandstone blocks** and **smooth sandstone stairs.**

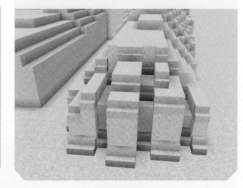

STEP 47

Build a frame like this for the outline of the head. You can play around with the shape of this frame until you are happy with it.

STEP 48

Use the frame you've just created to fill in the back section of the head. Look at the picture to see how it curves outward.

STEP 49

Use more of the same blocks to flatten off the front of the head. It should now look like this!

STEP 50

Then, create this shape on the front of this flat surface. This will be the outline of the face.

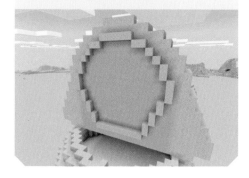

STEP 51

Build out, like this, to create a frame for the bottom of the face.

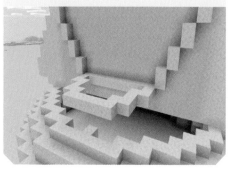

STEP 52

Now fill in the face. Build up the layers making sure each new layer is a little smaller than the one below.

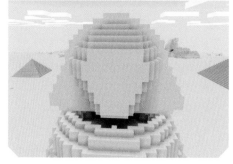

STEP 53

Add the facial features using **smooth sandstone blocks** and **smooth sandstone stairs**.

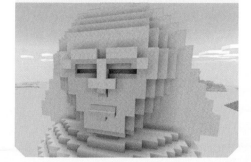

STEP 54

For the base of the tail, make this shape in the center at the back.

STEP 55

Add more blocks and fill out the tail, so that it wraps around the back legs, like this!

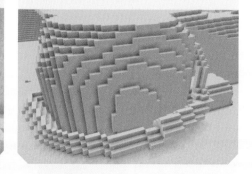

BLOCK GUIDE

Here is a list of all the blocks you'll need to build your Ancient Wonders.

Egyptian Obelisk

- Chiseled quartz blocks
- Sandstone blocks
- Smooth sandstone blocks
- Sandstone stairs
- Smooth sandstone stairs
- Cut sandstone blocks
- Chiseled stone brick blocks
- Chiseled sandstone blocks

Karnak Temple

- Cut sandstone blocks
- Quartz brick blocks
- Smooth sandstone slabs
- Smooth sandstone blocks
- Smooth sandstone stairs
- Sandstone blocks
- Chiseled sandstone blocks

Abu Simbel

- Chiseled red sandstone blocks
- Cut red sandstone blocks
- Red sandstone blocks
- Red sandstone slabs
- Red sandstone stairs
- Smooth red sandstone blocks
- Smooth red sandstone stairs
- Red sandstone fencing
- Armor stands
- Leather armor

Parthenon

- Quartz brick blocks
- Smooth quartz blocks
- Smooth quartz stairs
- Quartz pillar blocks
- Armor stands
- Iron armor

Lighthouse of Alexandria

- Quartz blocks
- Quartz stairs
- Stone blocks
- Armor stands
- Iron armor

Colossus of Rhodes

- Stone blocks
- Green concrete blocks
- Lime concrete blocks
- Dark prismarine blocks

Giant Wild Goose Pagoda

- Stone brick blocks
- Stone brick wall blocks
- Stone brick stairs
- Gray wool blocks
- Andesite blocks
- Andesite stairs
- Birch wood plank blocks

Great Wall of China

- Stone brick blocks
- Stone brick stairs
- Cracked stone brick blocks
- Mossy stone brick blocks

Forbidden City

- Smooth stone blocks
- Red concrete blocks
- White terracotta blocks
  Glazed orange terracotta
- blocks
- Jungle planks blocks
- Jungle planks stairs
- Polished andesite stairs
- Lanterns
  Crimson fence

Olmec Stone Head

- Stone stairs
- Stone slabs
- Cobblestone blocks
- Cobblestone stairs
  Cobblestone slabs

Pyramid of the sun

- Light gray terracotta blocks
- Granite blocks
  Granite stairs

Machu Picchu

- Dirt blocks
- Grass blocks
- Cobblestone blocks
- Cobblestone stairs
  Mossy cobblestone blocks

Great Pyramid and Sphinx

- Smooth sandstone
  Smooth sandstone stairs